ROLF'S
WALKABOUT

ROLF'S
WALKABOUT

Carol Serventy and Alwen Harris

PHOTOGRAPHY
Vincent Serventy and Rolf Harris

RIGBY LTD

We would like to thank John Cameron of the Australian Broadcasting Commission, Sydney, for getting the whole show on the road and Cathy Garland for making sure nothing we needed was forgotten.

Carol Serventy and Alwen Harris

First published 1971
Reprinted 1971
Reprinted 1972

This edition published by
A. H. & A. W. Reed Pty Ltd.
for Rigby Ltd., Adelaide.

ISBN 0 589 07092 4

Designed by William Mobbs

Set in Linotype Optima by Dover's Pty. Limited, Melbourne
Printed and bound by Dai Nippon Printing Co. (International) Ltd., Hong Kong

Ayers Rock

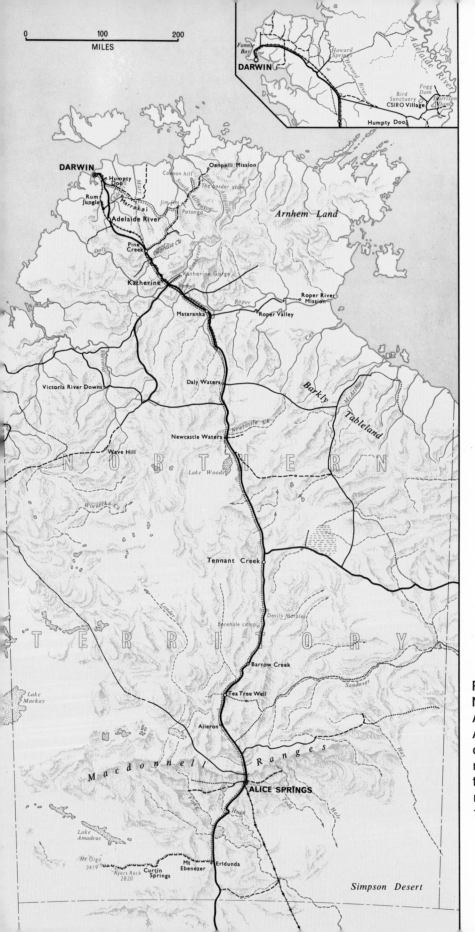

Rolf's walkabout in the Northern Territory of Australia, from Darwin to Alice Springs with the odd exploration off the main track. The route taken is outlined on this map — a two month, 1500-mile safari.

Contents

Plans and preparation

ROLF FLUNG HIS legs over the side of the chair in our sitting room, grinned through his beard and said,

'How about all of us having a camping holiday in the bush next year?'

A marvellous idea, we thought, and pressed him for details. Rolf had to give two concerts in Darwin in May of the following year, and after that was taking a three months holiday.

'I can't think of a better idea than going camping with you lot,' he said. 'You know all about it.'

Our 'lot' is Vin, a naturalist and writer, myself and our three children, Karen twelve, Cathy ten and Matthew five. Our family is certainly used to camping. Vin has made many desert expeditions, filming and writing about Australia's wildlife, and the whole family has camped in the bush in Western Australia many times. Our longest trip took us six months!

In 1965 we left Perth on the west coast with a caravan and a four-wheel drive vehicle and travelled fifteen thousand miles round the north of Australia to Sydney on the east coast, filming wildlife all the way. We spent a lot of our time away from our caravan, camping out. The results of this trip were twenty-six half-hour wildlife programmes for television, and a book, *Nature Walkabout*.

Rolf wanted to travel south from Darwin to Alice Springs and Ayers Rock, a distance of about one thousand miles.

'We'd like to sleep out in the bush, cook all our own food and really see the country. No hotels or motels,' said Alwen.

'You'd better see it soon,' Vin said, 'because unless the government creates National Parks out of the millions of square miles up there, and puts in rangers to look after them, there'll be nothing worthwhile to see soon.'

We had explored all this area in 1965 and felt that this wild and beautiful country, and its wildlife, should be captured on colour film. Vin, as an ardent conservationist, wanted to show the people of Australia the wonders of the Northern Territory, and show them why it should be preserved in its natural state.

Obviously, a good way to do this would be to make colour films of what Rolf and his family would see on a holiday guided by an expert bushman and naturalist.

Rolf, intensely interested in his country and in the Aboriginal people who live in the Northern Territory, couldn't have agreed more.

So it was decided that Vin should put the idea of a television documentary, 'Rolf's Walkabout', to the Australian Broadcasting Commission. In it we would try to show what any tourist could see and do in Australia's wild tropical north and in the central desert.

Rolf and I went to school together in Western Australia, and at one time Vin was one of Rolf's science teachers. Another ex-pupil of Vin's, and an old friend of Rolf's, is Harry Butler.

'What about seeing if Harry can come?' Vin said. Harry, a naturalist, animal collector and experienced bushman, had been on many trips with us before.

'Good idea,' said Rolf. 'I'll leave it to you to fix everything.'

May 1969

And so, a year later, Vin and Alan Bateman, the ABC director, flew to Darwin to meet Rolf and Alwen and their four year old daughter, Bindi, and to look over the country. The children and I were to join them two weeks later.

As luck would have it, Harry, with a party of American scientists, was driving up to Darwin from Perth, collecting fish for the American Museum of Natural History, and would arrive the same month, complete with all the stretchers, mattresses, tents, sleeping bags and cooking gear the Harrises would need, and all ready to spend the next two months with us.

The organisation in Sydney was fast and furious. Cathy Garland, the ABC's wonder-girl, and I made lists and lists and lists.

To keep the expedition mobile and flexible Vin wanted the ABC crew to be as small as possible. This meant three men only, who would have to make camp, cook and look after themselves as well as working hard all day, every day, filming. Cathy and I drew up long lists of food, first-aid equipment, camping and cooking gear, and bush clothing they would need, then Cathy had the job of buying and packing it all! Added to all this were the duplicate sets of the complicated filming and recording equipment. Cathy and I inspected the loaded long-wheel based land-rover 'Knobby' Clarke, the camera man, and Ron Moore, the sound recordist, were to drive from Sydney, up through Queensland and across the Barkly Tableland to Darwin. There wasn't a square inch to spare.

'Where on earth are they going to fit all the food you'll be buying them in Darwin?' Cathy said to me.

'Well, they've got our tent, stretchers, sleeping bags and cooking gear. When we have taken these out they'll have some room.'

I was kept busy organising clothes for Vin, the children and myself. We needed cool things for the tropical heat of Darwin and plenty of warm clothes for the freezing night temperature of Ayers Rock. I knew everything would have to be hand washed in basins with river or creek water and nothing would be ironed while we were away. We all needed six sets of identical shirts, shorts and jeans, for continuity in the filming. So much easier not to have to remember what you were wearing the previous day, especially where the children were involved.

Letters discussing all these things flowed back and forth between ourselves and Alwen and Rolf in London.

Cathy and Matthew got permission from their headmistress to take two months off school and I collected written work for them from the Correspondence School. The headmaster of Karen's High School gave me a serious look and said, 'I think you should take along a tutor for Karen — I'll be available for the position.'

'Can you cook?' I asked him.

At last all was ready. We flew off in the cold drizzling rain from Sydney at 7am and stepped out of the plane in Darwin in the steamy heat of the afternoon. Rolf, Alwen, Bindi and Vin were there to meet us. The walkabout had begun.

Bindi and Matt in search of Aboriginal paintings.

◁'Tie Me Kangaroo Down Sport'. Rolf meets the famous marsupial, the red kangaroo, in central Australia. Once familiar in the inland plains, numbers have been severely depleted by hunters in many areas.

Karen and Cathy examine a 'compass' termite mound near Darwin.

Alwen studies her first native cat. We trapped this native cat for filming. Although flesh-eaters and looking something like a domestic cat they are marsupials and are still common in northern Australia.

Possums can make good pets and various species are found in all parts of Australia, even in the cities. Carol introduces herself.

Vin's job was to film intimate wildlife shots which could be later cut into the rest of the film. Photographing nature takes considerable time and patience, and a knowledge of your subject. Vin waits in the shadow of The Olgas for a pied butcher-bird to come within camera range.

Australia's only stork, the jabiru. This stately bird is common across the whole of the north and is strictly protected.

Darwin and Howard Springs

'ONE MORE CONCERT,' Rolf said, 'and tomorrow we can move out to Howard Springs.'

That night we drove out in the cool beautiful moonlight to the Botanic Gardens. We passed hundreds of people, families, children, babies in pushers, all carrying rugs and cushions and cool drinks, and steadily walking along the road leading to the entrance. We could hardly push through them with the car to deliver Rolf to the stage. Almost everyone in Darwin must have been there.

A huge white moon hung poised over our heads as Rolf bounded on to the stage for three hours of laughter and song.

Rolf very generously gave all the proceeds of his Darwin concerts to a project to enable Aboriginal children to board in Darwin and attend High School.

We had collected our four-wheel drive Toyota vehicle from the Commonwealth Department of Supply and packed in our gear. Suddenly Karen and Cathy shouted, 'Here's Harry!' as they saw a dusty landrover, pulling a trailer and with a boat perched on its roof, hung all about with water-bags, cans of petrol, axes and shovels, pull up to the motel door.

Bindi and Matthew danced in excitement around the new arrival, then with the ABC crew we set off for Howard Springs, a small national park, seventeen miles south of Darwin. Howard Springs was our trial camp before 'Walkabout'.

A shady spot near the creek which ran from a pool was chosen for the camp site and all the children helped Vin, Rolf and Harry unload the vehicles. Stretchers were set up, everyone arranging their own

16

mattress, pillow, sleeping bag and mosquito net.

Bindi was thrilled with her white Arab-shaped tent, with a zip-up door, and invited Matthew in to play. There was just room for two stretchers, a suitcase and Bindi's collection of books, toys and coloured felt pens. Matthew's tent was dark green and had room for three stretchers. We all intended to sleep under the stars but the tents were there in case of rain and as places to dress.

Then it was time for a swim. The beautiful pool was fringed with black wattle trees, and at one end were water lilies. As the pool was very deep, Bindi and Matthew wore floats on their backs and rubber flippers on their feet. Rolf or Vin kept a close eye on them.

'Look, Harry!' Bindi pointed to a tree, whose trunk leaned out over the water.

Harry swam over, reached out and picked up a snake. It was about three feet long and an attractive green colour. Everyone swam up to look and he said, 'It's a tree snake. Lovely little thing, quite harmless. Like to hold it?'

'Won't it try and bite us?' asked Bindi.

'No, it lives on small animals, geckoes, lizards or birds. It looks for its food in trees—you're too big. Anyway it's not poisonous,' answered Harry.

'Can it swim?' asked Cathy.

'Hold it till I get my camera,' said Vin.

Cathy let it go after it was filmed and it swam sinuously towards the bank.

On one side of the pool was a tiny patch of rain forest, about a quarter of a mile long and 100 yards across. We all put on long trousers, long sleeves and socks, rubbed our faces with insect repellent to protect us from being eaten alive by mosquitoes, and went for a walk through the green tangled forest. We picked our way over and among fallen logs, the buttress roots of huge trees and tried swinging on the hanging lianas, like Tarzan. Rolf was very good at this.

All around us blue butterflies fluttered from branch

to branch, and far above we could just make out the black leathery folded wings and little fox-like heads of the fruit bats, hanging upside down. The rain forest was beautiful and very peaceful with its little creek wandering through.

Walking back to camp, on the edge of the rain forest, we found a muddy hollow where some large animal had obviously been enjoying itself splashing around.

'A buffalo wallow,' said Vin.

'I wish we could see a buffalo,' said Matthew.

'We'll see hundreds when we get further down the track,' said Vin, 'but I saw three early this morning, standing just there in that long grass, and tomorrow I'll bring you and Bindi over to see if they're there again.'

Next morning Bindi woke Rolf very early. She shook his shoulder and pulled at his beard until he opened his eyes.

'Come on Daddy! We're going looking for buffalo.'

We walked quietly along the track skirting the patch of rain forest. Everything was still and fresh in the early morning. Suddenly a harsh laughing-bird call, loud and long, startled us. Vin told us it was a blue-winged kookaburra and held out his binoculars to Karen.

'What a noise,' said Bindi. 'I wish I could make it.'

'Ssh—there they are.'

Three grey bulky buffaloes with spreading horns turned their heads and gazed at us. Everyone stood still, then the buffaloes turned and lumbered into the forest.

'They're very tame, just like cows,' said a dis-appointed Matthew who was hoping to be charged by a savage buffalo.

Vin told us that a wounded or sick one might be dangerous. 'You'll probably be able to get close enough to get a good photograph when we're in the Jim Jim area,' he said to Rolf, who always had his camera at the ready.

'Jake the Peg' delights a Darwin audience. However, Rolf was in for a shock some weeks later when he sang the same song for an audience of Aboriginal children. They flew in all directions in sheer terror. This strange three-legged, black-coated creature couldn't be their old friend Rolf?

19

◁'Me Rolf!' Australia is not all desert. The patches of lush monsoon rain forest near Darwin provide a naturalist's haven. Twining lianas snake up to the sky in search of sunlight — ideal for Rolf's Tarzan act.

Howard Springs, our first campsite. Here Rolf was able to wash off the dust. During the last war a small creek, fed by springs, was dammed to make a forest fringed swimming pool. Rolf and the children spent more time in the water than out of it and here Rolf taught Bindi and Matthew to swim.

Most snakes are not dangerous; a nature lesson from Harry. He shows that the tree snake can be interesting and even beautiful, rather than terrifying. These reptiles climb among the trees in search of frogs, their main diet. Their teeth are solid and they have no poison glands.

'Walkabout' does not mean that school is forgotten. Harry reads to Bindi and Cathy, while the other children work elsewhere.

A beautiful spiny spider. This spider has a harder skin than most, providing protection from its predators. Spiny spiders spin orb webs in low bushes and feed on the mosquitoes of the monsoon forest.

A walk in the morning sun. Ron records a 'wild' sound track to be used in the film while Rolf and Bindi talk over the plans for the day. Bindi enjoyed this kind of walkabout but Rolf had other ideas.

Early morning hair plaiting. Rolf helps Cathy plait her long hair. Karen stands by keeping a critical eye on the work. Her short hair was obviously more practical for bush travelling.

Deep in the rain forest a shaft of sunlight shines through a gap in the tree canopy and reaches the forest floor. The forest provided a cool shelter from the blazing midday sun.

The tree frog, food for the tree snake and freshwater fish. A frog that Rolf tried to release in the water crawled out onto the land, time after time, determined that the dangers of dry land were less than those of the water.

Fannie Bay beach

ALAN BATEMAN, the director, wanted to film everyone at a beach, so lunch for the whole party was packed into cartons and put into Harry's landrover. Vin reminded us all to take sunburn cream and hats. It was going to be a very hot day.

After driving about twenty miles north-west, we turned off the main road on to a widening dirt track. Huge rain forest trees grew thickly on each side and met at the top, forming a shady archway. Coming out of this patch of forest into a clearing of long grass we saw the remains of a long abandoned wooden house. Three coconut trees planted there long ago swayed in the breeze.

Harry drove his landrover under one of the trees, climbed up on the roof and dislodged some green coconuts with his handaxe. As they bounced on the ground the children raced for them. With a quick cut the tops were sliced off and soon everyone was drinking the coconut milk. It was delicious, clean and clear, it tasted like a nonfizzing lemonade.

'Ah! That's good,' said Karen. 'I wouldn't mind being shipwrecked on a deserted island as long as there were plenty of coconut trees full of coconuts.'

Behind the house were old fruit trees and beyond them a creek. The rain forest jungle surrounding this clearing was slowly recovering its ground. We walked out of the sunlight into the forest.

'It's like being underwater,' said Karen. 'All green and weird.'

'Ouch!' suddenly came from Alwen. 'There's something in my hair.' She shook her head and brushed some bright green ants from her head and back. 'Aren't they beautiful? They look like little emeralds.'

Gazing up we saw, hanging just above our heads, a

football sized nest of leaves with green tree ants scurrying all round. Vin reached up and pulled two leaves apart. Worker ants immediately rushed to the hole and, lining up along the edges of the leaves, began to pull them together again. Holding one leaf with their hind legs they leaned across and gripped the other with their jaws. Sometimes two or three ants would make a living chain to close the gap.

Slowly the leaves moved together. Then as they touched, a worker hurried up holding an ant grub in its jaws, clasped about its middle. It was moved from side to side, a fluid coming from the grub's mouth being used to stick the leaves together. When the grub ran out of fluid it was returned to the nursery and another carried up.

Rolf held Bindi up so she could watch.

A commanding shout from the film crew at the landrover hurried us back.

Fannie Bay beach, with its golden sand and sparkling blue water, and fringed with pandanus trees and she-oaks, stretched before us.

'Look! Mudskippers.' Vin led the way to where the outgoing tide had left runnels of water and soft mud. He told everyone to stand still.

We stood stock-still, looking like statues, and after a moment little flicks and jumps revealed dozens of mudskippers, leaping up to ten or twelve inches across the sand.

Cathy pounced, then opened her hand. A brown, three-inch long fish with large frightened eyes in a square face looked up at her, then with a flick of its powerful little tail, was gone.

'Not too many fish can climb trees,' said Vin. 'This one climbs the mangrove roots and quite enjoys being out of the water.'

By now, everyone's eyes had become accustomed to finding them and mudskippers were seen every-where—clinging to the muddy rocks and flicking over the water.

Nature is a great sculptor. Here, three cup fungi grow on a dead branch which Bindi and Matthew brought back to the camp. Rolf thought they would make an interesting ornament for their home in London, which is where they are now — branch and all.

One morning a freshwater tortoise walked into our Howard Springs camp! These reptiles are known as sideneck tortoises, since they cannot pull their long necks into the shelter of their shells, and fold them under, sideways. They are flesh-eaters, catching fish, freshwater crayfish, frogs and other small animals.

Fannie Bay, Darwin. The milky blue of the northern waters is caused by the fine silt stirred up by the tidal movements. During winter these beaches provide excellent swimming, though in summer swarms of stinging jellyfish send swimmers to freshwater pools, such as Howard Springs. The trees in the foreground are pandanus, palm-like tropical plants, sometimes called screw-palms or screw-pines because of the screw-like way in which their leaves grow from the stem.

28

◁ Picked when green, coconuts contain a refreshing lemonade-like fluid instead of the familiar coconut milk. Rolf thoroughly enjoyed this drink during breaks in the filming. Matt and Cathy were suspicious at first but soon agreed that 'coco-ade' was great. Coconuts are not native to Australia but were introduced by early white settlers.

Rolf shows Bindi and Cathy a hermit crab peering out of its shell.
These crabs have specially shaped abdomens for gripping the insides of their shells. Because their shell home protects them, they do not have the usual heavy crab armour, though their claws and the front of their bodies are hard.

Mudskippers, fish that are more at home out of the water than in. Their enlarged gill covers, keeping their gills moist, enable them to survive out of the water for some time. Mudskippers even climb up mangrove roots in search of food.

To the joss house

AS SOON AS the filming of the mudskippers had finished, Rolf and the children dashed out for a swim.

After a picnic lunch, sitting on the sand in the shade of the mangrove trees, we all walked a few hundred yards along the beach to a spot, just at the edge of the bush, which Vin and Harry wanted to show us.

It was a huge mound of leaves—like a little hill. Harry carried Bindi and we all climbed to the top.

'What do you think we're standing on?' said Vin to Karen and Cathy.

They were mystified.

'Could it be a nest, Dad?' said Cathy.

'Right. A fowl's nest. The jungle fowl scratches up this huge nesting mound and the eggs inside are kept warm by the heat from the decaying leaves until they hatch.'

We scrambled down the slope of loose dry leaves and headed back to the water. It was so hot that everyone wanted to swim every few minutes, then come out and see what was being filmed, or see what animals they could find at the water's edge. Bindi found a shell walking along under the water. Karen took it and placed it gently in the palm of her hand.

'It's a hermit crab. Just . . . a minute . . . and . . . you'll see him.'

Then a tiny head with stalked eyes and quivering feelers slowly poked out of the shell. When Karen moved her hand, the crab disappeared suddenly, then it slowly re-appeared and waved its feelers in the air.

Soon everyone was hunting hermit crabs and with squeals of delight Matthew and Bindi picked them up, waited for a sight of the crab, and then carefully put them back on the wet sand.

We decided to look at the Joss House on the way back to camp. The Joss House was built by the Chinese living in Darwin and is open all day to visitors. Two stone lions, each with a stone ball in its mouth, guard the entrance. Matthew and Bindi loved them and tried for ages to get the stone balls out of their mouth. They were naturally puzzled how they got in in the first place.

Inside, sticks of incense scented the air. Around the walls were scarlet and gold dragons, and fascinating Chinese figures with elaborate head-dresses and long drooping black moustaches. Above some decorated tables holding little bowls of rice were green, gold and scarlet embroidered silk hangings.

'I feel as though I'm in China, don't you?' whispered Cathy to Karen.

It was difficult to persuade Bindi and Matthew to leave the stone lions.

After the drive back to camp everyone felt like a swim. Rolf was teaching Bindi to put her face down in the water and swim to him, kicking with her flippers. Then Matthew had a lesson from Rolf.

Back at camp, the soup was simmering and the steak sizzling on the campfire.

The four children had been swimming all day and were happy to tuck in their mosquito nets and relax on their stretchers as soon as it was dark. The rest of us sat around the campfire peacefully sipping our mugs of hot coffee. The film crew came across from their camp site and we all decided to make a very early start the next day to film the water-birds at Fogg Dam, about forty miles away south-east.

'We must be there in time to see the sun rise,' said Vin firmly.

Everyone groaned.

Inside the Joss House at Darwin the decorations were gay and exotic. The sweet odour of incense was everywhere.

The temple was adorned with Oriental statues. On the table below them were gifts from worshippers.

Two stone lions, with balls in their open mouths, guard the doors of the Joss House. Bindi and Matt did their best to remove one of them but the skill of the carver beat them.

Matthew riding on one of the stone lions.

Not a heap of leaves but a huge nest. A bird called the jungle fowl scrapes up soil and leaves to make a giant incubator in which its eggs are buried. The chicks, on hatching, push their way to the surface and fend for themselves, without help from their parents. *Below:* Hermit crabs shelter under logs or leaves during the day and by night search the floor of the forest for food, even a loaf of bread from our camp table.

Cycads are an ancient group of plants, perhaps among the most primitive of seed producing plants. The round seeds were important food for the Aborigines. Raw, the seeds are poisonous but by grinding them, then washing with water for a day or so before cooking, they are edible.

Herons gathering for a feast at Fogg Dam. For some reason thousands of small cat-fish were swirling in the drain and hundreds of pied herons and egrets came to the feast. Whiskered terns had to dip down to scoop up the small fish while their long billed rivals snapped up the fish.

Fogg Dam and termite mounds

AS WE DRIFTED off to sleep, a few leaves floated down on to the mosquito nets. These dark green oblong-shaped nets, ex-army, are slipped over four steel poles about three feet high, which are driven into the ground at each corner of the stretcher.

We woke to find a mug of hot tea on the ground beside us, the fire lit and the smoke drifting slowly up. Harry had awoken ahead of us all again!

By the time all the cameras, film, hats, sunglasses, food, drink and children were loaded into the vehicles, the sun had beaten us too. But it was still early in the morning, about 7am. Fogg Dam is a small earth dam built by the CSIRO as part of an experimental rice cultivation project. It was later abandoned.

As we walked along the road into the dam area, we disturbed thousands of birds. Egrets, magpie geese, burdekin duck, white ibis, pied herons, pygmy geese and jabiru made a glorious sight as they all flew over us to gradually settle back to feeding on each side of the road.

The water lily leaves made a carpet over the water of the dam and delicate lotus birds ran across them, all legs and toes as they stepped lightly from leaf to leaf.

Harry discovered a 'cat-fish boil' in a channel and called the children up to see it. The dropping water level had caught hundreds of cat-fish in a pool and they were leaping up out of the water. We crouched down and caught the fish in our hands.

The film crew kept their cameras whirring. Ron, our sound-recordist, who wasn't long out from England, couldn't get over the sight of the thousands of magpie geese feeding so close to where he was recording.

Next morning, Rolf wanted to see the termite

mounds Vin and Harry had described to him. We drove a few miles back along the road towards Darwin, parked under some shady trees and walked about half a mile through the bush to where the 'tombstones' were. About twenty termite mounds, around twelve feet in width and eight feet high, but only two feet thick, dotted the grass flat. The ground was dry, but in the 'wet' season it would be very swampy. The north of Australia has only two seasons, the dry winter, which is the only time for tourists, and the wet summer.

The broad side of these termite mounds always faces east and west, and the thin edge north and south, consequently they're called 'compass' termites. The whole mound works like an air-conditioning unit. With one side always in sun and the other in shadow, there is a flow of cool air to keep the insects' stored food dry in the wet season.

The children wanted to go back to Howard Springs with Rolf and Vin for a swim, so Harry drove us into Darwin to buy the last of the fresh food and stores we needed to take along the track. What a list! Twelve people for two months. For a start we needed 120 tins of fruit and 120 tins of fruit juice! Back at Howard Springs it was sorted into three lots and stowed away in the three vehicles.

Harry rigged up a bed for Bindi behind the front seat of his landrover. She stowed her sleeping bag, pillows, books, and dolls there so she could read or sleep in comfort. The back seat of the Toyota was removed so that it could be loaded with food, cameras, kitbags and equipment. The five mattresses were laid on top of all this so Karen, Cathy and Matthew could also lie flat and sleep during the day's travelling.

After a week at Howard Springs we were keen to get on the road. First thing in the morning we headed for the East Alligator River, the eastern border of Arnhem Land, and our furthest point east.

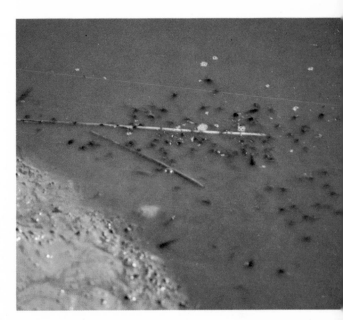

A 'boil' of cat-fish. These freshwater fish are common in the pools and rivers in this area. On this particular day, as they rose to the surface in great swarms, they had the misfortune to be preyed on by numerous water-birds.

Fogg Dam was built to supply water for an experimental rice growing project. The industry failed for a number of reasons but not, as was generally thought, because of bird-pests. However, the dam was not wasted, it is now an important sanctuary for birdlife. Thousands of pied geese come to feed on the plants which grow in the swampy soil and the area has become one of Darwin's tourist attractions.

41

Vin leans on a 'compass' termite mound, the home for myriads of termites. The mound is extraordinary in that it is built in slab-like fashion, the broad sides facing east and west, and the narrow edges pointing north and south. This produces an air-conditioning effect, with one side always in the sun and the other in shadow providing a flow of cool air through the mound.

'Compass' termite mounds rising above the long grass. Here you can see their distinctive east or west, flat sides.

Rolf's hat made a good sun-shade for Bindi and Matthew. The rest of us had to be content with the shade from the termite mounds, giving us relief of about 10° in the 90° temperature.

To Jim Jim Creek

WE DROVE EAST over the Marrakai plains, where the black soil was dotted with feeding buffalo. Rolf was anxious to film them but Vin said, 'Wait till we get to Jim Jim. There's plenty of buffalo there.'

We drove for hours, until suddenly around a bend in the dusty road we saw the South Alligator River.

'We'll have to stop here,' said Harry, 'and cut some bamboo to float the trailer across.'

'Fine,' said Alan Bateman. 'We'll film it.'

The children were pleased when we decided to camp here. Hanging over the river was a huge, lazy, drooping gum tree and Bindi and Matthew spent the rest of the afternoon playing in it.

Harry had cut down some long bamboo poles to make his floats and, thinking that some bamboo mugs would be useful, we asked Harry to saw off six mugs. Each was about eight inches tall, the base being the node of the stem. They were perfect for drinking water from.

It was a beautiful place to camp. That night we lay on our stretchers looking up at a sky crowded with the stars. 'You can't do this in London,' Rolf and Alwen commented.

The next morning we watched the film crew wade out into the river, holding their equipment high above their heads. They set up the camera on the other bank, ready to film us making the crossing.

There was great excitement as the vehicles slowly churned through the water to the other bank. Safely over, Harry stopped to remove the bamboo floats from the trailer and then we all drove on towards Jim Jim.

Since leaving Darwin we had passed many road signs pointing to Jim Jim. For Rolf, the words had taken on a magical quality. He pictured a cowboy town with one long street and people coming into the General Store for supplies. He got a shock when we finally arrived to see a river with the sign, 'Jim Jim Creek', and alongside it a building on stilts with a long set of concrete steps leading up to it. This shop sold sweets, tinned food, beer and petrol.

The next day we went fishing in Jim Jim Creek using Harry's flat-bottomed boat, which he kept on top of his landrover. Harry caught a huge barramundi, which we cooked and shared out.

We camped beside a billabong, near Patonga. This lovely stretch of water was fringed by paperbarks and across the water we could watch egrets at their morning fishing. This is also the site of Don McGregor's safari lodge.

The next day we were lucky to have Don McGregor as a guide. He said he'd show us the most likely spots where we would see the wildlife of the area —around the lagoons and off the track. We couldn't have had a better guide. Young and quietly spoken, Don has explored this area for twenty years, and once spent six months on horseback in rugged Arnhem Land.

Sandy McGregor, Don's wife, cooked us an early breakfast of magnificent buffalo steak and we set off. The sandy track crossed creek beds and passed turn-offs to such places as—Dreaming Waters Lagoon, Nourlangie Rock and Munmalary Station.

We drove past a group of station outbuildings and the airstrip of Mudginberry Station. A small plane was drawn up at the front door of the homestead. About twenty miles further on—

'Turn here,' directed Don and we left the road. Before us was a green plain, covered with hundreds of grazing wild buffalo. Beyond them we saw a green wooded parkland and a huge outcrop of rock.

45

Matthew, Bindi and Rolf enjoying their dip at the crossing. Later, with the aid of soap and flannels we turned the swimming pool into a bathroom: hair-washing time.

Alligator River crossing. This made a marvellous swimming hole for the children while we worked out how to get our vehicles across without wetting the cargo. Huge paperbark trees fringed the river.

47

◁ Vin and Nobby were not the only cameramen. Rolf was also an addict and the coloured leaves of this tree provided an attractive close-up. The Australian bush is not only sombre grey-green it is often alive with varying colours and forms.

A herd of water buffalo. These animals were introduced from Timor in 1825, and flourished. Today they are hunted, mainly for meat, and as a result have become fairly timid. Today, about one hundred thousand buffaloes roam on the plains between the East Alligator and Adelaide Rivers.

The buffalo is a formidable looking animal. No tourist has ever been attacked by one, but wounded or old animals may be dangerous. Recent research has shown that the buffaloes are destroying waterlilies and other water life, and causing erosion by their feeding and other behavioural patterns. It seems likely that the buffaloes may have to be destroyed in the new national parks being set up.

49

◁Dreaming Waters. During the wet summer, when fifty or so inches of rain may fall, the coastal plains to the east of Darwin become a vast sea of water. During the 'dry', the flooded plains dry out but many beautiful pools like this one remain.

Rolf's camp at Jim Jim. Harry's land-rover carried a vast amount of gear, including a boat. A lean-to tent provided shelter against rain, mosquitoes and sandflies so the Harris family had all the comforts of home—well almost!

51

Camp near the East Alligator. This beautiful country, apart from the grazing herds of buffalo, resembled a vast park. Since our walkabout the Government announced that a thousand square miles in this area will be set aside for a national park.

The escarpment country. This high ridge of country rises from the plains and contains thousands of spectacular Aboriginal cave paintings. Much of this land is Aboriginal reserve.

Giant termite mounds looking like small huts. They can reach twenty feet in height and weigh many tons. Each mound provides security for hundreds of thousands of grass eating termites.

Vin carried a lot of gear on the roof-rack of the Toyota. Bindi and Matthew were always there to help unload.

Making camp. Bindi and Matt doing their share. Every one helped and after the first few days we could make camp in about twenty minutes.

At Cannon Hill

'THIS IS CANNON HILL,' he said and walked on, bare-footed, towards the rock.

Under a big, projecting overhang of rock we saw the whole face of the cave brilliantly coloured with Aboriginal paintings. Many were X-ray paintings, only found in this part of Australia, showing the internal organs of the fishes, kangaroos, turtles, tortoises, geese and other animals depicted in red and yellow ochre.

We sat on the stone, which was shiny and polished from the rubbing of countless Aboriginal bodies and listened as Don told us about the Ibieri people who had lived here.

Behind us stretched a beautiful grassy plain, thickly wooded, with the edge of the plateau looming in the distance.

The longer we looked at the paintings the more animals and objects we saw. Matthew was most excited when he found a drawing of a gun. Harry told him it was an old flintlock. A little distance away was a long flat piece of rock face. Along it danced seven fighting men, drawn like stick figures, in white ochre. These hunters were holding loaded spear throwers with barbed spearheads and feather ornaments. One held a spear and a goosewing fan, and had feather decorations at his elbows. These were the most lively and exciting paintings in the cave and we kept coming back to look at them again and again.

The next day we returned to Cannon Hill with the film crew. Alan decided that he would need several days to film the paintings and naturally we were glad to be able to camp a while in this peaceful park-like valley.

Morning and evening the children pestered Rolf for Perro (a "Spanish" dog-fish puppet character created by Rolf). They were delighted when Rolf finally said, 'All right, go and get him.' Perro puppet sat on Rolf's hand, with the four children seated in front of him expectantly. Within a few seconds all attention was centred on that naughty, rude, misbehaving, very funny dog-fish. A swift dialogue between Perro and Cathy finished with Perro begging for some crumbs of biscuit and Cathy eventually getting him a biscuit, breaking it up and throwing the crumbs into his mouth. Rolf himself had almost disappeared, and the completely new and different personality of Perro had taken over.

Harry is a wonderful camp cook and very inventive with ordinary ingredients. Every morning, Karen would watch Harry cooking breakfast and have a cooking lesson at the same time. She learnt to make 'johnny cakes,' Harry's pancakes, of every conceivable kind. Add a tin of fish and you have a savoury breakfast, add something sweet and you have a sweet breakfast. After eating breakfast at our campfire, the children would go over to Harry and scrounge whatever he could offer them. As a result of this they ate very well! Usually we cooked separately, as five people are enough to cook for on one campfire, but sometimes Harry would combine his talents with ours to produce a magnificent three course meal.

Harry shot wild pig and made delicious stews and curries and, sometimes, we were given wild buffalo steak by the station people. This steak is beautiful, full of flavour and very tender.

Bread keeps for a long time in plastic bags, but when it did run out Harry made us 'damper' from self-raising flour and water. He would rake the coals away from the fire, then bury the loaves, wrapped in aluminium foil, in the hot sand. In the morning the foil was unwrapped to reveal delicious hot bread.

55

Here we found one of the most beautiful galleries of Aboriginal art we had ever seen. The rock-ledge floor below the gallery shone like glass, polished by human bodies: the bodies of the painters as they worked here over the years. The hollows on the rock-floor indicated where red and yellow ochres were ground to powder to form colour pigments.

Some of the paintings were obviously of recent origin. Matthew found one depicting a musket. Guns appeared frequently in this gallery, showing the impact this powerful weapon had made on the Aborigines.

Don McGregor has lived in this country for twenty years. He has walked over much of it, travelled by packhorse and by four-wheel drive vehicles. Today he runs a tourist guest centre, 'Patonga', for adventurous travellers. Carol and Cathy listened attentively to his stories of the outback.

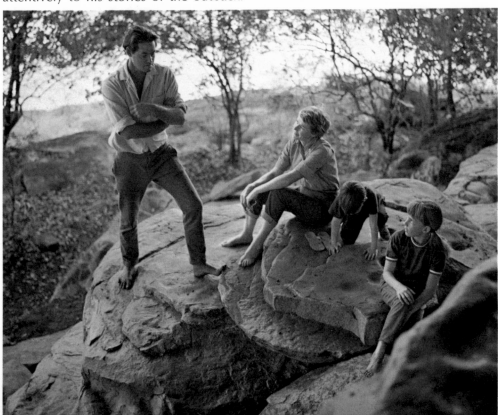

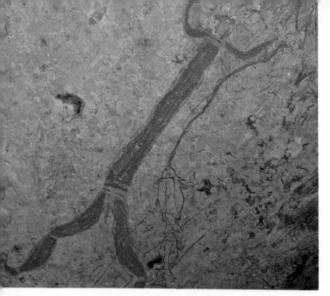

A hunter with a string of fish. Such paintings often had magical significance, with the hunter becoming more successful in the painting than in reality.

This is the country of X-ray paintings. ▷ Here the artist shows not only the outside but some of the internal organs of the animal. In this case the paintings are of the barramundi, favoured fish food of the area.

More gun paintings. As guns came into the hands of the Aborigines they became proficient in their use. Extra magical powers could have been added by their depiction in this gallery.

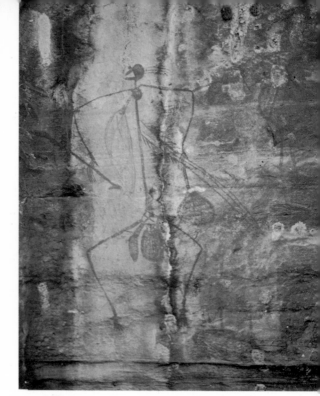

An archer fish knocks down its victim, a spider, with a 'spit' of water. This fish is able to spit water in this manner using its specially shaped mouth.

A longnecked freshwater tortoise in X-ray style. This kind of painting is found only in this area of Australia.

A spirit figure carrying fighting spears and his dilly bag. Goose feather quills decorate his elbows.

Another sorcery painting. Without an initiated Aboriginal guide it was impossible to find the real story behind these magical figures.

A curious Rolf. These superbly drawn 'mimi' figures show hunters, some holding spear-throwers with barbed spearheads and feather ornaments. The hunter on the left has feather decorations on his elbows, holds an additional spear and a goose-wing fan. Another has a dilly bag slung from his shoulder, the way the men usually wear them. Drawn over the hunters are two female figures with long legs and pointed toes.

A painted hand. Stencils of handprints are a feature of cave paintings throughout Australia.

Rolf delighted the children with his hand puppet Perro, the Spanish dogfish. Perro kept the children enthralled with his rough and ready character, full of quick and rude wit. After breakfast or before dinner Rolf produced Perro. All of us were

drawn into the Perro magic. Constant dialogues took place between Rolf, Cathy, Bindi and Matthew and Perro. If any of the adults dared to leave Perro's presence without permission, he called them back to order.

Wandie Creek

WE HAD FINISHED filming the cave paintings, so it was time to break camp and move on.

On the last morning, we drove back two miles to 'The Border Store', a wooden shed-like building with a wide verandah, built under the shade of a huge tree. Terry Robinson's store must be one of the most isolated in the world. His customers, mainly Aborigines from the Oenpelli Mission, walk the eleven miles from the mission on the other side of the river to buy food, soft drinks and brightly coloured dresses and to sell him bark paintings.

We were pretty proficient at loading and unloading the vehicles by this time. Before starting, there would be kitbags, stretchers, clothes, cameras, chairs, tables, food, cooking utensils, tents and odds and ends strewn around, but somehow everything fitted into its place. The children climbed into the vehicle last, stretching out on the mattresses to play games, read or sleep until our next stop.

We turned west for the Stuart Highway. The film crew's landrover was very heavily laden with filming equipment and we went slowly over the sandy patches to make sure they would get through safely. With Harry's landrover in the lead and ours in the rear, we sandwiched them in the middle, so they could be either pulled or pushed out if they became stuck.

However, we made the bitumen road without any trouble. Katherine Gorge, about 300 miles south, was to be our next main filming place, but on the way we called in to see Vin's two nephews, John and Peter, who, with their wives, are pioneering a tin mine at Wandie Creek, about 150 miles from the Gorge. After a long hot and dusty drive it was a joy to relax in their living room, which was perfectly designed for the hot, dry climate. It was separate from the kitchen, standing all on its own, and consisted of a roof, a smooth cold concrete floor and four walls of wire mesh. Vines and creepers were growing thickly up wire trellises outside each wall. Inside it was cool and airy, sheltered from the hot sun by this thick tangle of green leaves. A wonderful collection of native tools, stone axe-heads, flints and stone knives and beautiful old bottles lined the room.

Dry creek beds, with soft white sand, are always favourite places to camp, and John and Peter directed us to a perfect camp site.

That night we had a barbecue for everyone and after, sat around with our coffee while Peter and Lyn, John and Angela told us of their life away from civilisation. Rolf was occupied chipping out bowls from pieces of wood. As we talked we could hear his chisel working away. The immense star-filled sky and the quietness of the bush for miles around, emphasised the feeling of isolation from civilisation. The flickering light of our campfire soon made us drowsy and we stumbled off to bed.

A few minutes later, Alwen felt a movement next to her stretcher and put out her hand. Into it walked a baby crocodile! She cried out in excitement. Everyone got up and crowded around to look at and hold it. It was a freshwater crocodile, about a foot long and harmless to man, as they feed only on fish. Startled by so many people it started making a high pitched sound, something like a kitten. We stowed it away safely for the night and next morning everyone's camera was out to film it walking from pool to pool.

'Let's keep it,' said Bindi.

'No fear,' said Rolf, and he filmed it as it rapidly made off for the next pool. It wasn't going to waste any time in getting away from us.

Pancakes for breakfast. It is cold in the early morning in winter. While the breakfast cooks on the fire, Cathy suggests that Rolf provides breakfast music on a section of plastic pipe — modern type didgeridoo, the drone pipe of the Aborigines.

At a billabong camp site. 'That one Cathy,' says Rolf. The fresh-water lagoons of the north have a rich growth of colourful waterlilies. Unfortunately, buffaloes are destroying these delicate plants in many areas.

Freshwater crocodile. This reptile was once common throughout northern Australia but excessive hunting reduced their numbers drastically. It is now a protected animal in Western Australia and the Northern Territory but not in Queensland.

Alwen caught a young freshwater crocodile as it walked past her camp stretcher one night. We were camped in a dried creek and the crocodile must have been looking for a bigger pool. Next morning Harry showed Karen its sharp peglike teeth. Rolf was content to keep his distance. Freshwater crocodiles can grow to six or seven feet long but are harmless to humans. They feed on fish and other small animals.

68

Katherine Gorge

JOHN HAD RIGGED up a very neat shower arrangement, using the creek water, and we took turns in indulging in long cold showers. The top and bottom quarter of the room was open all round and while showering we could watch tiny lizards sunning themselves on the warm rocks.

We would have liked to stay longer and film Peter and John's collection of old bottles and Aboriginal tools but the film crew had already dashed on to Katherine and we had to follow.

Two wheel tracks over the ground were our only guide as we wound our way round trees, termite mounds and rocks, travelling so slowly we could easily see the small animals scurrying off the track as we approached. It took us two very relaxing hours to travel the thirty odd miles to the main road—then it was fast driving along the bitumen to reach Katherine.

It is a small dusty town with one wide main street. We stopped to buy fresh bread and meat, newspapers and to collect the mail waiting for us at the post office. Then we pushed on the twenty miles to Katherine Gorge, and made an early camp.

About a mile before the Gorge, Harry suddenly braked his landrover, jumped out and streaked off into the scrub. His keen eyes had seen movement, and he had not wasted a second.

He came back with a magnificent nine-foot long black rock python. These snakes are not poisonous and kill their food, rabbits or small wallabies, by gripping them with their jaws, flinging their coils around them and exerting such a strong pressure that they suffocate. Bindi and Matthew squatted quietly around it, quite at ease. Their confidence came mainly from Harry's attitude. He explained everything about the snake to them. Had there been any danger, he wouldn't have allowed them anywhere near it.

We filmed the snake on the dusty road where it was easy to see its track.

'It's got no legs,' Matthew suddenly said.

'It lifts small sections of itself forward with its muscles,' Vin explained.

We were lucky to have seen this snake as most snakes in the Australian bush are timid and move out of your way before you see them.

For hundreds of years the floods of the great Katherine River have carried down sand and boulders, and spread them in a great tumble across the surrounding plain. Each flood brought down layer after layer and as time passed they hardened and formed the rocks of the beautiful Katherine Gorge which the river winds through now. Today it is still carving away at this rock and carrying it further downstream.

We were all looking forward to spending the next day on the river. A twenty-foot, flat-bottomed boat was ready to take us up the gorge first thing in the morning.

This is a national park and no shooting has been permitted here for the past four years, so we were able to see lots of crocodiles basking in the sun on rock-islands, some water dragons also sun-baking and small water snakes swimming purposefully from one rock to another.

When we came to a small rapid or waterfall, we left our boat and wound our way through the boulders to the next pool. Another boat was waiting there to carry us further down the river.

On the way back we saw our biggest crocodile of the day, nearly seven feet long. The boatman slowed the engine and we chugged gently past him. Then with an explosive swish he was gone, swimming fast for the bank.

Pythons are not poisonous. They kill ▷ their victims by constriction (ably demonstrated by Rolf), gradually squeezing their prey to suffocation and then swallowing it in one piece — even a duck or a possum. We saw few snakes on our trip as these reptiles are very timid and keep out of harm's way.

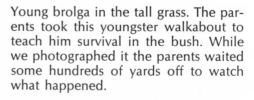

Young brolga in the tall grass. The parents took this youngster walkabout to teach him survival in the bush. While we photographed it the parents waited some hundreds of yards off to watch what happened.

We taught the children commonsense about snakes. Many are harmless, like this rock python, and the dangerous ones will only attack if frightened or if accidentally stepped on.

Overleaf
The very beautiful Katherine Gorge. The river has carved a pathway through the soft sandstone and conglomerate rocks, aided by the natural breaks in the rock structure. The whole area is a national park and the river provides one of the best places to see freshwater crocodile, which through strict protection have become very tame.

Bamyili

WE WERE EAGER to reach the Bamyili Welfare Settlement where the Aboriginal children were going to dance a children's corroboree for us, so the next day we drove back through Katherine and the sixty miles south on to Bamyili that night.

We camped about four miles from the settlement and went in early the next morning. Passing the houses and gardens where the staff live, we pulled up outside the school, set in large grassy grounds. Across the road, Matthew and Bindi spied the kindergarten building with lots of swings and slides and play equipment outside. Their reaction was automatic and quick as a flash they were inside swinging and sliding.

We followed them and were welcomed in by Wendy Neale, the teacher. She showed us the paintings the children were doing and asked Bindi and Matt if they'd like to join in. *Would they?* They were delighted, and were soon surrounded by an excited group of smiling faces.

During our tour we saw some laundry tubs and a clothes line and tentatively enquired if we could do some washing. We had had no chance of washing any clothes since Howard Springs, 15 days ago and things were getting really desperate.

Mrs Neale said, 'You can use my washing machine over at the house'.

We left Matt and Bindi painting, drove back to our camp and collected up bags and bags of dirty clothes. We washed all day and hung up line after line of clean clothes, the hot dry wind drying everything in a few minutes. With great satisfaction we took our piles of clean, dry clothes back to the camp.

Meanwhile, the men of the party had been making arrangements for the children's corroboree and Rolf had had a reunion with his friend David Bulanatzi, a superb didgeridoo player who some years ago had flown to London to appear with Rolf on his BBC TV show.

The school children and teachers all gathered round on the grass to watch the corroboree. Two boys, one of them David Bulanatzi's son, danced for us, to the music of three didgeridoos. The deep rhythmic note of the didgeridoo and the very skilful dancing of the boys recalled the rich traditions of the Australian Aborigines.

Rolf decided to give a concert himself, to say 'Thank you' to the children. He disappeared inside the school and changed into his three-legged Jake the Peg costume. There were wild screams of delight when he emerged, microphone in hand, singing. As he approached each group of children, they scattered before him like leaves in the wind, squealing with excitement, (and the young ones in fear) at this three-legged monster. The men of the tribe, standing at the back, tried to look a little dignified at all this 'children's business,' but were soon roaring with laughter.

The old women and the young women with babies, at first very shyly sitting a long way away on the grass, gradually came closer and closer as the children clamoured for song after song.

The teachers organised a delicious cold buffet lunch for us all at the Home Science Centre and in the afternoon the film crew, Harry, Rolf and Vin went off to film the men dancing.

Our camp was near an old tin mine and each morning and evening we fossicked around the old workings for long forgotten 'treasures'. Bindi and Matt found masses of treasure, lumps of rock, old screws, bits of tin, great heavy iron bars—all of which we had to carry back to camp and lose at some later date when they had forgotten them.

Bamyili Welfare Station was our first stop south of Katherine Gorge National Park. Here Rolf was to meet an old friend, David Bulanatzi and his family. David had flown to London to take part in a *Rolf Harris Show* and to show his skill on the didgeridoo. Here David's son and a school friend showed that talent runs in the family as the boys danced for us. It was all part of an entertainment provided by Rolf for the schoolchildren, and by the children for us.

In the afternoon the men performed a dance spectacle for us: a corroboree. This was only a 'play' type dance as the sacred corroborees could only be performed before initiated men. Here the men paint themselves in traditional fashion for the dance. The paints were not traditional however, being poster paints

The leader of the dance. He was the stage manager who organised the pattern and played a major part in all the dances.

The dance-leader armed with spears, points with his spear-thrower in the long grass. This was part of the goanna dance and told of the Dreamtime and of a hunt for the goanna.

Here, the dancers armed with spears take their part in the goanna hunt. Often in 'play' corroborees amusing incidents of the day's hunt may be mimed for the amusement of the men, women and children.

Two other dances were performed for us. One showing the coming of the white man and with him disease and tobacco. The making of fire using a fire-drill was part of the performance.

◁ David Bulanatzi.

The orchestra. Two didgeridoos and two clapping sticks provided the rhythmic background for the dancing.

Bamyili to the Devil's Marbles

WE WERE UP before dawn next morning as Rolf and the camera crew had to meet David on a little hill nearby where they would be filmed playing and singing *Sun Arise*, as the sun actually rose. David came back to our camp for breakfast and afterwards played his didgeridoo for us.

Harry made pancakes—everyone's favourite and, towards the end of the trip, the only breakfast the children would eat. Into a big bowl would go eggs (if we had any), self-raising flour, powdered milk, sugar, and currants or sultanas, and from the frypan would come hot, delicious but very filling pancakes which we would smother with butter (if we had any) or golden syrup.

With the bush all round us, the wood smoke curling up from the fire, the harsh calls of the crows as the sun rose higher in the sky, the strong pulsating music from the didgeridoo held us spellbound.

It was sad leaving Bamyili. The vehicles were all packed up ready to move when, during a last minute poke round the old mine workings, someone threw a rock down a mine shaft. There was a far-off splash and suddenly thousands of bats were flying up and out, skittering around the trees and back down the various openings of the old mine—bats were flashing everywhere. We watched in amazement as it was so sudden and there were so many of them.

'We must film this,' said Rolf, so we unpacked all the filming gear and set up the cameras. Harry unpacked some mist nets—very fine nylon nets—and placed them across an opening of the shaft. We wanted to trap some bats in these fine nets so they would not hurt themselves and could be filmed close-up.

They are fascinating creatures. In the air, their silent flight and black leathery wings make them frightening to look at but close up their soft furry heads and large lustrous eyes were quite attractive. They can fly and hunt in pitch darkness by echo-location, sending out sounds at very high frequencies and 'seeing' by the echoes.

After this excitement to finish off our three day stay at Bamyili, we re-packed the equipment and set off for the Devil's Marbles.

We camped by a billabong just past Newcastle Waters and were excited to find thousands of budgerigars wheeling in the air, down and up, down and up, towards the water. Seven or eight times the flock of birds skimmed the surface of the water and went up.

'They're thirsty,' said Vin, 'but they're land shy. In the flock the dazzle effect helps to keep them safe from birds of prey.' He pointed to a tree at the edge of the soak where a large brown hawk and a black-cheeked falcon were sitting motionless, waiting. We took turns to look at them through the binoculars. 'As soon as they settle and drink, it's easy for the falcons to pick off the weaker ones.'

Mid-afternoon the next day we passed the Devil's Marbles. This collection of giant red granite boulders is strewn over acres of country, as if tossed down by a giant hand. The road winds through the centre of them. Many of the boulders are quite round. We were nearing the centre of Australia where the desert nights are very very cold and the days extremely hot. These extremes of temperatures have caused rocks to expand and contract, and peel away in layers.

As soon as we had stopped, the children were up and away, rock climbing with gusto, while Vin and Rolf went off with cameras to film spinifex pigeons. We looked for small animals, but, after lifting dozens of small rocks all we found were a few geckoes, it was too cold and too dry to support much animal life.

Firemaking. A thin cylinder of wood is spun rapidly in a hole in a piece of wood. The friction of the spinning breaks off bits of burning dust which fall into tinder held below the hole. The glowing tinder is then dropped onto a ball of grass which, hopefully, bursts into flames.

David Bulanatzi. ▷

Rolf, with clapping sticks and David with didgeridoo play music around the campfire.

Termite mounds. Not all are huge but these occurred in thousands along the Roper River bank. The insects feed on the dead
grass.

We set a trap for animals for filming and here Harry shows a
native cat to Rolf and Alwen. All animals were released after
filming.

Pink lotus. This waterlily is famous in Asia and northern Australia and is the sacred lily of Buddha. Its seeds, stalks and underground runners were used as food by the Aborigines.

Freshwater pools were always an attraction. Many had a number of varieties of waterlilies blooming. These plants are found mainly in the tropics though many have been introduced into home gardens around the world. The flowers are large and the main colour of the ones we saw was blue.

'The Alice'

WE CAMPED at a borehole not far from the Devil's Marbles. Boreholes have fascinating names like Muckety, Spinifex Bore, Cabbage Tree Bore and Afghan Bore, and comprise windmills for bringing water to the surface and water troughs for the stock. There is usually some overflow so the small area around the borehole often has more trees, shrubs and wildflowers than the nearby country, and of course, at dusk, the birds—brolgas, galahs and pigeons—flock to the water.

For an ornithologist, the most exciting thing that can happen is to rediscover a lost bird. Vin lost no opportunity to search for the 'night parrot'. This is a green ground parrot that has not been seen by knowledgeable naturalists since the turn of the century, but they believe it still survives in this desert country.

Many nights, Vin contrived to get to a borehole to camp, as the parrot drinks at night. Even if the country round a borehole was windy, dusty and treeless and we all groaned at the sight of it, Vin insisted on camping there. No chance for a sight of the night parrot could be lost. Unfortunately, we had no luck on this trip.

At last we were nearing Alice Springs, the 'heart' of Australia and nearly a thousand miles from Darwin. By this time we had travelled nearly two thousand miles, with all our excursions off the main track.

The countryside had changed from the lush tropical rain forest of Howard Springs, through scrub land to desert. The country we were travelling through now was sparsely covered with saltbush and other shrubs, and the brown rocks, red sand and bright blue sky made startling contrasts. These contrasts were accentuated by the very clear air and bright colours found in the desert.

'The Alice' is a colourful town, lively and friendly. Its wide main street is thronged with stockmen, Aborigines, townsfolk and tourists. The wide dry sandy bed of the Todd River winds through the town, fringed with huge old river gums. Groups of Aborigines often sit and talk on the sand in the shade of the trees. Perhaps every five or six years heavy rain will cause a flash flood and the Todd will flow. The Macdonnell Ranges, just north of the town, wind away in the distance.

We drove through Alice, then through a gap in the ranges, called Heavitree Gap, to a park-like bird sanctuary bounded on one side by the Todd River. Here, at Pitchi-Richi, an old friend Leo Corbett, had prepared a place in his bushland section for us to camp. Tents up, beds ready and campfires built, we joined Leo and his wife, Elsa, in a walk around his outdoor folk museum of old mining equipment, buggies, displays of Territory minerals, opals and Aboriginal implements.

Birds were everywhere. Leo provides food, water and trees for the birds, so there were pigeons, galahs, parrots, willy wagtails, honeyeaters, finches and miners, flashing through the trees and feeding on the sugar he sprinkled on the terraces outside his home.

The next day we packed lunch, picks, chisels and spades, took plenty of water and followed Leo's land-rover about five miles out of the town, over a bush track, to an old gravel workings.

There we fossicked around and found traces of an amethyst lode. Harry dug a hole and revealed a vein of amethyst running down the hillside. In fact, rough amethyst pieces were all around us. We just sat on the ground quietly searching for the crystals or digging with small picks and shovels to find bigger lumps. Crystal after crystal was washed in a bucket of water, admired, and put away in a calico bag to take home.

Around us on the hillside were spectacular red and orange craggy boulders and, in the distance, over a yellow dusty plain, the beautiful Macdonnell Ranges.

91

Budgerigars at a waterhole. As we moved further inland we began to see small flocks of budgerigars. At Newcastle Waters one morning about twenty thousand birds came to drink. Some drank from the edge, some came down onto the water and hovered like tiny green helicopters.

92

A dead tree springs to life as budgerigars gather on it. Then the 'leaves' drift away again as the birds take flight.

In this dry country water can be obtained by drilling into artesian basins below the surface. The intake beds for these wells are many hundreds of miles to the east. Once tapped, the water pours to the surface under pressure. Here two brolgas take an afternoon drink.

The Devil's Marbles. These huge granite boulders glow red in the afternoon sun. The action of the sun, rain and wind over thousands of years has shaped them into these rounded tors.

A close-up of the Devil's Marbles with sharp pointed spinifex grass in the foreground. The original granite of the rock was traversed by joints and giant cracks which allowed rain to penetrate and help weather the rocks into these giant boulders.

Morning tea at Pitchi Richi. Leo Corbett, the owner of this sanctuary at Alice Springs, had prepared a camping site for us. Rolf provided some morning tea music while Leo tried to record it on tape.

The Todd River at Alice Springs is lined with giant river gums. These provide roosting places for thousands of galahs—known as rosebreasted cockatoos in Europe. They are the comedians of the bird world.

Plumed pigeons. These delicately coloured inhabitants of the rocky ridges of central Australia came to Pitchi Richi for the seed that Leo provided. Hunger satisfied, the birds would rest in the shade.

Miners, a kind of honeyeater, came to take sugar from feeding table.

The resting female pigeons were often disturbed by courting males who, full of passion, displayed their plumage vigorously before the apparently bored female birds.

Bindi and Matthew at breakfast. Often, slices of bread and honey were stolen by the miners who watched carefully from the bushes nearby.

Pure quartz is colourless but with impurities it may occur in a variety of colours. The gemstone amethyst is a purplish wine colour.

Afternoon sunshine turned the sand quartzite hills nearby into patterns of golden spears and tall pinnacles. The children were interested only in their climbing qualities.

Bindi and Matthew go hunting for gemstones and other oddments just waiting to be picked up. By the end of the trip they had gathered a good collection.

Striking it rich! This cut in the red earth revealed masses of amethyst on a weathered vein. Some were small, some were middle sized and some were large. Every now and again there would be a cry of delight as one of us 'struck it rich'. By the time we left the amethyst vein even Bindi and Matthew had bulging bags.

Henley-on-the-Todd

OUR NEXT FILMING trip was to the Old Telegraph Station, now a National Park. Its stone postmaster's residence and telegraph station have been beautifully restored. The telegraph station was built in 1872, at the site of a waterhole called Alice Springs. A town was built later, two miles away, and named Stuart, but in 1933 it was renamed Alice Springs.

The ranger showed us kangaroos and emus that lived in a large fenced area of bush. One emu was sitting on his large glossy green eggs and another was shepherding his brood of tiny striped chicks through the bushes. Father emu does all the work of hatching the eggs and looking after the young until they are about eighteen months old. All the mother has to do is lay the eggs. An excellent system, we thought.

David Howe, whom we had met on our previous trip to the Northern Territory, told us he had some three-week-old dingo pups out at the Animal Industries Branch. We drove out to see the museum there and to look at the research work they were doing. Matthew and Bindi fell in love with the beautiful soft little pups. The dingo is the wild dog of Australia. Originally, the Aborigines used them to hunt for food, as well as keeping them as pets, but now they roam wild in all the outback areas, a problem to pastoralists as they kill sheep and lambs.

Every spring, a Henley-on-the-Todd Carnival is held at Alice Springs. This hilarious day has mock life-saving, yacht races and water skiing on the *dry* bed of the Todd River. The barefooted crews, dressed as pirates or clowns, clutch their boats and run the races on the sand. Rolf went along to start some of the races. It was fun for all. So far, rain has never ruined the day by putting water in the river.

Evenings around the campfire at Pitchi-Richi were a delight. In Leo Corbett, Rolf met his match as a story-teller and he told story after story of life in the outback in the old days—he had us all in fits of laughter.

When we were exhausted from laughing Rolf played the accordion and sang. Leo's stories were laced with memorable phrases: of an old swaggie, 'In the morning his eyes were stitched up with red cotton' and of a transceiver radio needed in the desert, 'It couldn't pick up a buzz from a blowfly two yards away'.

From Alice Springs there are endless interesting places to visit. The Ooraminna Rocks, some twenty miles from Alice Springs, have been decorated with hund-reds of engravings—drawings picked into the red rocks by Aborigines centuries ago. In the claypan surrounding the rocks we found many Aboriginal tools, little flints and pieces of hard stone they had shaped to make scraping or cutting instruments.

·A place of sacred significance to the Aborigines was Emily Gap, in the Macdonnell Ranges a few miles east of Alice Springs. On one side of the gap the rock face is carefully painted with red and white lines and dots. These are sacred paintings of the witchetty grub totem, and at this rock face, called 'the decorated eyes', the ceremony to ensure the increase of the totemic animal was carried out every year. Witchetty grubs were an important food source for the Aborigines. These paint-ings are still very clear and colourful though it must be many years since the ceremony was performed and the drawings repainted by the Aborigines.

There were only ten days before our planes left Alice Springs to return us to Sydney, and Ayers Rock was still two days' drive away.

Emu and eggs. The mother emu lays the large dark green eggs and then the father takes over and incubates them. When the chicks hatch the father looks after them for about eighteen months.

From another nest two chicks had hatched. Cathy and Karen hold the prettily striped chicks for Bindi and Matthew to see.

Rolf faces the female emu. The male sat ▷ firmly on the eggs while his mate followed Rolf around. This reversal of roles is unusual in nature.

◁ 'Tie that kangaroo down,' was Rolf's cry as a big red began to spar with him. These animals prop themselves up on their powerful tail, grasp with their arms and then jump forward with their strong back legs, using their large tearing claws to tremendous effect. If annoyed, a big kangaroo is strong enough to cause severe injuries to humans.

Mountain or thorny devil. This is one of the dragon lizard family and is harmless, feeding entirely on small black ants.

Dingo pups at Alice Springs. The dingo is the wild dog of Australia and in the outback country it has become a major problem, killing sheep, lambs and even calves. These dingo pups belong to the research station at Alice Springs.

Henley-on-Todd. Perhaps not the traditional idea of a Henley Regatta but in central Australia most rivers are permanently dry and only flow after heavy rain. This 'yacht' is propelled by human legs rather than wind, similarly, rowing boats are propelled by sand scoops wielded like oars while the boat runs on rails.

Emily Gap, to the east of Alice Springs, is another reserve. Here rock paintings cover the rock face on the lower levels.

Standley Chasm, a few miles to the west of Alice Springs, is a tourist attraction and reserve. At midday the rocky gorge glows with brilliant colour as the sun shines in.
The colour fades to a low-key brown and red when seen with the sunlight falling from behind the photographer. After floods, this gorge is a torrent of water.

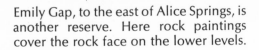

Emily Gap paintings. The long lines of ▷ red ochre painted over the white clay background represent witchetty grubs. The dots are the eggs of the grub. These insects were an important food of the Aborigines and each year the grub symbols were repainted and appropriate ceremonies carried out to ensure that the witchetty grubs would multiply to feed the people for the coming year.

Overleaf
Ayers Rock. This road between Ayers Rock and the Olgas shows how the water runoff along the road edge encourages more vigorous plant growth and the trees here grow taller than usual.

Ayers Rock

THE LAST STAGE of our journey (the trip out to Ayers Rock) was also to be the most exciting. We had to plan our food, water and petrol supply most carefully, as there were no supplies of food or water and only one stop for petrol on the three hundred or so miles from Alice Springs to The Rock. The state of the roads was never very good and if heavy rain fell, it would be impossible to get through. We anxiously watched the clouds that were gathering. We felt we should be all right with our four-wheel drive vehicles but a delay of two or three days would cut short our filming time.

We drove south on the Stuart Highway and turned west towards Ayers Rock. At the roadside was a huge sign warning travellers to carry ample supplies of food, water and petrol. We would pass two station properties where petrol was sold at the homesteads, Mount Ebenezer and Curtin Springs, but knowing that bad roads and boggy conditions could increase our vehicles' petrol consumption, we were well prepared.

On the first night out we camped in a sheltered grove of wattle trees. It looked as though rain might fall during the night so we put up the tent and put as much under cover as we could. Next morning the ground around us was firm, so we set off happily. .

We passed a group of Aborigines with their camels. Once the Aborigines walked everywhere but now there are so many wild camels in 'the Centre', left over from the days when they were used as pack carriers, that they have taken to using them for getting around. The camels were feeding on the high branches of the mulga trees, pulling the branches down and tearing the leaves away. The big, unwieldy looking camel saddles lay on the ground near their campfires. We gave them some water, as they were short, and bought a small wooden goanna (lizard) which an Aboriginal girl had just finished decorating. With pieces of wire heated in the campfire she swiftly burnt the pattern into the hard yellow mulga wood.

As we travelled on we could see the square-topped, amethyst-coloured Mt Connor growing larger and larger and looking more beautiful. We stopped for petrol at Curtin Springs and on the dusty plain between us and Mt Connor we saw a flock of pink and grey galahs feeding on seeds on the ground. As we drove towards them they took off—first we were dazzled with a display of thousands of pink feathers massed together as they wheeled towards us, then grey as they turned and flew away.

We drove on slowly as there was a lot of water on the road. The centre was firm but the edges were very soft. We passed a tourist bus which had bogged at the side of the road, the passengers had obviously been taken on by other vehicles.

At last, in the distance, the first sight of Ayers Rock. Purple in colour and its shape unmistakable, we watched it for the last ten miles of the drive. For the Serventy family, Ayers Rock was like an old friend because we had spent ten days there in 1965. For Alwen, Rolf and Bindi, it was a new and enthralling experience. Every time Rolf looked at The Rock he took a photo of it as it changed its colour.

Its immense size, almost seven miles around the base, is hard to believe although you know you are looking at what appears to be the largest single stone in the world. The Rock was a sacred ceremonial place of two tribes of Aborigines and there are still many interesting cave paintings on The Rock. Some have faded through age and weathering, but some more recent ones, particularly in the Initiation Cave, are very clear.

111

Camels were brought to Australia in 1860 for use by the ill-fated Burke and Wills expedition. With the arrival of the motor transport they lost their value as beasts of burden in the outback and were turned loose to look after themselves. Today they thrive over most of central Australia, at times annoying station owners by damaging fences and water-troughs. Some Aborigines now use camels on their wanderings around the country.

A beautiful campsite on the dry bed of the Finke River. In the background are red hills dotted with rounded clumps of spinifex.

Mount Connor—a three mile long hill of quartzite to the east of Ayers Rock. After rain, the sand ridges surrounding it become a garden of wildflowers.

Galahs. These cockatoos are found throughout inland Australia and in recent years have become common in the cities. Like most of the parrot family, the beauty of their plumage is not matched by a beautiful voice, this being a harsh screech.

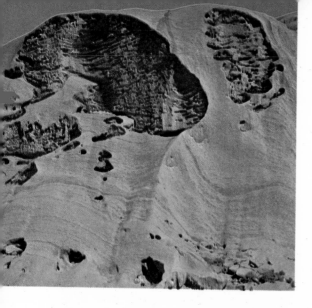

The Brain. This feature, etched into the rock surface by sun, wind and rain, was the place in the Dreamtime where the hare-wallaby people camped.

From a distance the summit seems smooth but when you reach the top you can see hollows, some holding small trees.

◁ Ayers Rock seen from the sandhills fringing it. These small hills were covered with wildflowers, tall desert poplars and other small trees.

◁ Flying over Ayers Rock. This unique rock is about a thousand feet in height, two miles along and five miles around the base. From the air, the erosion along the top and the sides can be seen clearly.

'Kangaroo tail' of rock. Here a huge slab of rock has been separated from the main mass by weathering.

Matthew draws pictures in the red sand of a desert dune. Each morning offers a new sand pattern from the movement of desert animals during the night.

The initiation cave of Ayers Rock. This huge rock has tremendous religious significance for the Aborigines. This particular cave was used only by men; women and children were forbidden to enter.

This cave painting in white clay shows the arrival of the white man. The horse was new to the Aborigines and the artist gave it a rather kangaroo-like appearance.

The moods of Ayers Rock. From the first rays of the early morning sun, through high noon, to the reds of sunset, the rock changes colour. A cloud passing over the sun can dull its colour to a pale yellow at sunrise. Then with the moving of the cloud it can glow golden. For most people it is the fiery reds of sunset which have the most appeal. At night it resembles a huge purple mass against the myriads of stars.

The Olgas from the air. This mass of rocky domes is some twenty miles to the west of Ayers Rock.

Many of the rocks of this outcrop are conglomerates or 'pudding stones', with huge boulders weighing several tons embedded in the main rock structure.

One of the many domes which make up the Olgas. This series of domes, Ayers Rock and Mount Connor are residuals left standing after erosion had worn away the rest of the rocks in the area.

The Olgas, looking like an Eastern city with blue domes and minarets, glow in the setting sun.

Rolf is duly impressed with his country's magnificence.

Our camp in the Olgas, on the edge of a small brook, received visitations from butcherbirds, but no other humans. We explored unheeded, after the 'comparatively populated' Ayers Rock.

Rolf's walked about

THIRTY MILES from Ayers Rock are the rounded domes of the Olgas. In the distance these appear to be mysteriously floating on the horizon, like the domes of some Eastern city. The explorer Giles named these rounded domes in 1872 after the Queen of Spain — 'an enlightened royal patron of science', in Giles' words.

We had permission to camp out there from the Chief Ranger (all this area is a National Park) and drove thirty miles to the Glen of Winds, a beautiful spot in the crevice of two rounded hills. A small stream flowed near our camp and we were able to draw water from a little pool. Matthew and Bindi gathered small sticks of wood to start the campfires and helped in setting up the camp.

The day after we arrived, some heavy black clouds joined us and we had the eerie sensation of seeing the top of The Rock disappear in swirling mist. Rain fell intermittently. Just enough rain fell to make a thin silver stream over the side of The Rock. We would race to the spot with cameras to try and film this beautiful sight, then the rain would stop, clouds would cover the sun and all would look grey again. The changing weather made it very difficult for the film crew but the coolness made it easier for us to rock climb and explore to our heart's content.

Every morning, as the sun came up, we would lie on our stretchers watching the rock face around us turn golden red. When the whole rock wall was glowing we knew it was time to get up and start breakfast.

The magpies and butcher birds visited us at breakfast time and as we threw them titbits they gradually ventured nearer and nearer. Their bird song is among the most beautiful in Australia and they gave us a chorus every morning.

Rolf's father and mother, Mr and Mrs Crom Harris, travelled all the way from Perth in Western Australia to Alice Springs, and then out to Ayers Rock by tourist bus to spend a few days with us. We all drove in from the Olgas to meet them and drive them round The Rock.

The last scene in our film series was to be a sunset campfire scene. About five miles from The Rock we set up a campfire on the road. People were stationed out of sight each side to stop any cars coming along who might run over us and just as the sun set, with The Rock as a background, Rolf began playing his accordion and singing. We all sang with him:

Pass the billy round, boys!
Don't let the pint-pot stand there!
For tonight we drink the health
Of every overlander.

as we passed around the mugs of tea.

As soon as the sun was down we packed up, went into the camping area near The Rock for our evening meal, then set up another campfire to complete the scene in darkness. We needed to use the electric light provided for the camping area so another campfire was built and our billy boiled up again on this one.

In the darkness, beyond the little circle of light, people gradually came to sit or stand and watch the scene being filmed. Rolf's father and mother were given seats very close and loved every minute of the filming. People staying at the tourist motels, campers, a busload that arrived that night and some of the National Park rangers strolled up and listened. Rolf entertained them all, his final song being *Jimmy, me boy*, which tells of an old Aboriginal passing on the wisdom of his tribe to his son.

To get the camera angles, the sound and the closeup re-takes right, Rolf sang it several times. For all of us, listening in the shadow of the great Rock, it was a glorious end to our two-months' camping holiday.

Bindi and Matthew come back with a load of firewood for our camp at the Olgas.

Cathy and Matt went rock climbing. The large 'raisins' in the pudding stone made the job a little easier.

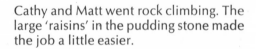

Cathy and Matthew at a freshwater pool in the Olgas. Towards evening this was a favourite drinking hole of the desert animals.

Rolf offers a helping hand to the rock climbers.

One of the Olga domes. Lines of weakness or joints allowed the weathering process to divide the whole rock mass into a series of isolated domes like this one. The highest dome is 2,600 ft. above sea level.

Boiling the billy. This is a traditional Australian custom where a 'billy' or metal can is filled with water and boiled over an open fire. Years of use turns the outside black. When the billy boils a handful of tea is thrown in, the billy whirled around in a number of circles and then the tea poured out.

Early morning. Alwen and Bindi lie snug in their sleeping bags while Rolf produces the morning tea. In the foreground is a huge heap of ash from the well-stoked fires, kept burning to reduce the chill of the desert night.

Reunion at Ayers Rock. Rolf's father and mother, Mr and Mrs Cromwell Harris, had come across from Perth to Adelaide, and then north for this meeting. Mr and Mrs Harris have driven around Australia several times so the outback was not new to them.

Rolf teaching all the children to dance to the tune of *Pass The Billy Round Boys*.

Overleaf
A misty cloud hung over The Rock behind Alwen and Rolf on our last day. A fine film of water over the whole mass turned it silver, a magnificent sight. Even though this country is desert, between five and ten inches of rain each year is the average. However, this does not mean that it rains every year· one drought lasted for seven years.